Contents

Schönbrunn Palace: view from the garden with the Great Parterre in the foreground

Central section of the façade facing the garden

I. General outline

With its long and at times momentous history, the imperial palace complex of Schönbrunn is one of Austria's most important cultural monuments. The whole ensemble, which includes the palace and its ancillary buildings, the park with its numerous architectural features, fountains and statues to-gether with the zoological garden, the oldest of its kind in the world still in use today, was added to the UNESCO World Cultural Heritage List at the end of 1996.

Owned by the ruling Habsburg dynasty since Maximilian II, the palace and its park and gardens were transferred to the ownership of the Republic after the end of the monarchy. In 1992 the Schloss Schönbrunn Kultur- und Betriebsges.m.b.H. was established as a modern, privatised management company and entrusted with the administration of the palace.

Imperial Pleasance and Deer Park at Schönbrunn; copper engraving by Georg Matthaeus Vischer, 1672

II. History

The history of Schönbrunn and the buildings that preceded the palace on this site goes back to the Middle Ages. The whole estate was known from the beginning of the 14th century as the Katterburg and belonged to the manor of the monastery at Klosterneuburg. Over the following centuries numerous lessees are documented, including a reference in 1548 to one Hermann Bayer, mayor of Vienna, who extended the property, transforming it into a substantial country estate.

In 1569 the estate and its manor house came into Habsburg ownership through Maximilian II. The contract of sale mentions a house, a water-mill and a stable as well as a pleasance and an orchard. This laid the foundations for a grand residence as well as for a pleasance and a deer park.

Following the sudden death of Maximilian II in 1576 the Katterburg passed into the ownership of Rudolph II, who merely provided the funds for its maintenance. Emperor Matthias used the grounds for hunting, and according to a legend while out on a hunting excursion in 1612 discovered the "fair spring" (Schöner Brunnen) after which the estate was subsequently named.

His successor, Ferdinand II, and the latter's wife, Eleonora of Gonzaga, both passionately fond of hunting, habitually chose Schönbrunn as the venue for their hunting parties. After Ferdinand's death in 1637 the estate became his widow's dower residence, and Eleonora, famed for her interest in the arts, led an active social life here. In 1642 she had a *château de plaisance* built here and it was at this time that the estate was renamed Schönbrunn, the name being documented for the first time in the same year.

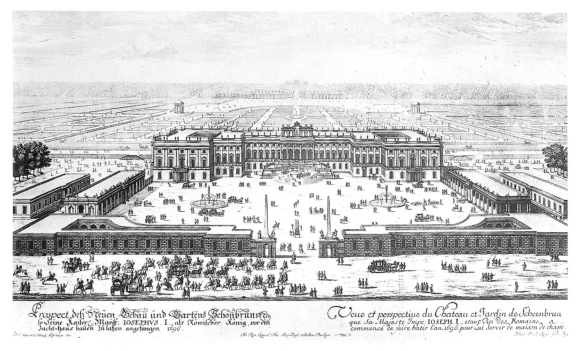

Second set of designs for Schönbrunn, copper engraving by Johann Bernhard Fischer von Erlach; built in 1696

In 1683 Schönbrunn together with its palace and deer park fell victim to the devastation visited on the area during the Turkish siege of Vienna. The property having passed into the ownership of Emperor Leopold I in 1686, the latter decided to have a magnificent new residence built for his son and successor, Joseph. Through the mediation of certain members of the nobility, the Rome-trained architect Johann Bernhard Fischer von Erlach was introduced at court. Having produced a first set of designs dedicated to Leopold I in 1688, he was engaged to teach architecture to the heir to the throne. In 1693 the emperor commissioned him to design a palatial hunting lodge, on which work began in 1696, partly upon the foundations of the *château de plaisance* that had been destroyed by the Turks. In the spring of 1700 the central wing of the palace was completed and ready to be occupied. The building of the side wings came to a standstill owing to financial difficulties resulting from the War of the Spanish Succession, and the remaining building work was abandoned following the sudden death of Joseph I.

Subsequently the unfinished palace was used as a dower residence again until Emperor Charles I acquired Schönbrunn in 1728 and eventually gave it to his daughter Maria Theresa.

The accession of Maria Theresa heralded an epoch of brilliance and splendour for Schönbrunn. Under the empress's personal influence and the supervision of her architect, Nikolaus Pacassi, the former hunting lodge was transformed into a palatial residence, assuming the appearance it still largely has today.

Work began with the extension of the audience chamber and residential quarters for the emperor and empress in the East Wing. This was followed by the demolition of the central perron or external stairs built by Fischer on the Parade Court side in order to create a spacious carriageway on the ground floor and construct the Great and Small Galleries on the *piano nobile*. In this first phase of remodelling these two grand reception rooms did not yet have their rich stucco decoration and ceiling frescoes. At the same time, the Blue Staircase was erected in the West Wing as a suitably imposing access to the *piano nobile.* The steadily increasing numbers of imperial offspring made it necessary to insert an intermediate floor between the *piano nobile* and the upper floor in 1748 in order to accommodate the children. A few years later an intermediate floor was also inserted in the West Wing.

Extensive ancillary buildings were also erected in order to supply the needs of the court household, which numbered more than 1,000 persons,.

On the express wish of Maria Theresa a palace theatre was built in the North Wing and opened in 1747.

In the second phase of rebuilding after 1753 the two galleries were given vaulted ceilings and embellished with magnificent stucco work and frescoes, thus creating a uniquely impressive Rococo ensemble. The majority of the rooms facing the gardens were decorated with the typically playful Rococo ornamentation known as rocaille, as well as mirrors and oil paintings set into the walls. Finally the Parade Court and garden façades of the palace were remodelled with the elaborate articulation and rich ornamentation so typical of the Rococo Age. Following the sudden death of Franz I Stephan in 1765, the widowed empress had several rooms in the East Wing of the palace remodelled as memorial rooms, sparing no expense. At almost the same time she had the so-called Bergl Rooms on the ground floor painted with exotic landscape murals.

Maria Theresa's last project, undertaken in the 1770s, was the laying out of the gardens under the supervision of the court architect Johann Ferdinand Hetzendorf von Hohenberg. He gave the gardens at Schönbrunn their architectural accent with the building of the Gloriette, the Neptune Fountain, the Roman Ruins and the Obelisk. The avenues, fountains and open spaces were enhanced with numerous statues and sculptures executed by Wilhelm Beyer and his workshop. The remodelling of the palace and its gardens was finally completed shortly before Maria Theresa's death in 1780.

Subsequently Schönbrunn remained unoccupied until the beginning of the 19th century, when Emperor Franz II/I used it as his summer residence. During his reign Schönbrunn was occupied twice by Napoleon, in 1805 and 1809. It was during this epoch too, between 1817 and 1819, that the court architect Johann Aman oversaw the removal of Pacassi's

Maria Theresa in oriental costume and mask; oil painting by Martin van Meytens, c. 1744

richly-decorated Rococo facade, replacing it with a plainer design with restrained ornamentation and having the façade painted in the shade today known as "Schönbrunn Yellow".

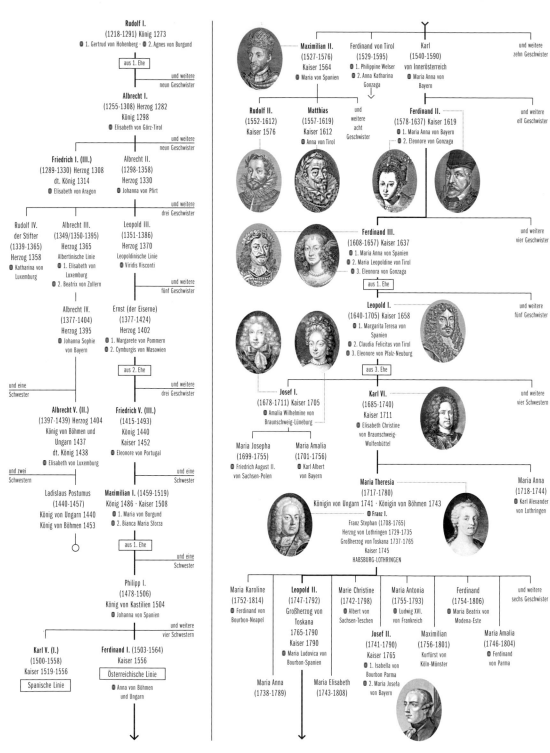

Rudolf I.
(1218-1291) König 1273
⚭ 1. Gertrud von Hohenberg · ⚭ 2. Agnes von Burgund

aus 1. Ehe

und weitere
neun Geschwister

Albrecht I.
(1255-1308) Herzog 1282
König 1298
⚭ Elisabeth von Görz-Tirol

und weitere
neun Geschwister

Friedrich I. (III.)
(1289-1330) Herzog 1308
dt. König 1314
⚭ Elisabeth von Aragon

Albrecht II.
(1298-1358)
Herzog 1330
⚭ Johanna von Pfirt

und weitere
drei Geschwister

Rudolf IV.
der Stifter
(1339-1365)
Herzog 1358
⚭ Katharina von
Luxemburg

Albrecht III.
(1349/1350-1395)
Herzog 1365
Albertinische Linie
⚭ 1. Elisabeth von
Luxemburg
⚭ 2. Beatrix von Zollern

Leopold III.
(1351-1386)
Herzog 1370
Leopoldinische Linie
⚭ Viridis Visconti

und weitere
fünf Geschwister

Albrecht IV.
(1377-1404)
Herzog 1395
⚭ Johanna Sophie
von Bayern

Ernst (der Eiserne)
(1377-1424)
Herzog 1402
⚭ 1. Margarete von Pommern
⚭ 2. Cymburgis von Masowien

aus 2. Ehe

und weitere
drei Geschwister

und eine
Schwester

Albrecht V. (II.)
(1397-1439) Herzog 1404
König von Böhmen und
Ungarn 1437
dt. König 1438
⚭ Elisabeth von Luxemburg

Friedrich V. (III.)
(1415-1493)
König 1440
Kaiser 1452
⚭ Eleonore von Portugal

und zwei
Schwestern

und eine
Schwester

Ladislaus Postumus
(1440-1457)
König von Ungarn 1440
König von Böhmen 1453

Maximilian I. (1459-1519)
König 1486 · Kaiser 1508
⚭ 1. Maria von Burgund
⚭ 2. Bianca Maria Sforza

aus 1. Ehe

und eine
Schwester

Philipp I.
(1478-1506)
König von Kastilien 1504
⚭ Johanna von Spanien

und weitere
vier Schwestern

Karl V. (I.)
(1500-1558)
Kaiser 1519-1556

Spanische Linie

Ferdinand I. (1503-1564)
Kaiser 1556

Österreichische Linie

⚭ Anna von Böhmen
und Ungarn

Maximilian II.
(1527-1576)
Kaiser 1564
⚭ Maria von Spanien

Ferdinand von Tirol
(1529-1595)
⚭ 1. Philippine Welser
⚭ 2. Anna Katharina
Gonzaga

Karl
(1540-1590)
von Innerösterreich
⚭ Maria Anna von
Bayern

und weitere
zehn Geschwister

Rudolf II.
(1552-1612)
Kaiser 1576

Matthias
(1557-1619)
Kaiser 1612
⚭ Anna von Tirol

und
weitere
acht
Geschwister

Ferdinand II.
(1578-1637) Kaiser 1619
⚭ 1. Maria Anna von Bayern
⚭ 2. Eleonore von Gonzaga

und weitere
elf Geschwister

Ferdinand III.
(1608-1657) Kaiser 1637
⚭ 1. Maria Anna von Spanien
⚭ 2. Maria Leopoldine von Tirol
⚭ 3. Eleonora von Gonzaga

und weitere
vier Geschwister

aus 1. Ehe

Leopold I.
(1640-1705) Kaiser 1658
⚭ 1. Margarita Teresa von
Spanien
⚭ 2. Claudia Felicitas von Tirol
⚭ 3. Eleonore von Pfalz-Neuburg

und weitere
fünf Geschwister

aus 3. Ehe

Josef I.
(1678-1711) Kaiser 1705
⚭ Amalia Wilhelmine von
Braunschweig-Lüneburg

Karl VI.
(1685-1740)
Kaiser 1711
⚭ Elisabeth Christine
von Braunschweig-
Wolfenbüttel

und weitere
vier Schwestern

Maria Josepha
(1699-1755)
⚭ Friedrich August II.
von Sachsen-Polen

Maria Amalia
(1701-1756)
⚭ Karl Albert
von Bayern

Maria Theresia
(1717-1780)
Königin von Ungarn 1741 · Königin von Böhmen 1743
⚭ Franz I.
Franz Stephan (1708-1765)
Herzog von Lothringen 1729-1735
Großherzog von Toskana 1737-1765
Kaiser 1745
HABSBURG-LOTHRINGEN

Maria Anna
(1718-1744)
⚭ Karl Alexander
von Lothringen

Maria Karoline
(1752-1814)
⚭ Ferdinand von
Bourbon-Neapel

Leopold II.
(1747-1792)
Großherzog von
Toskana
1765-1790
Kaiser 1790
⚭ Maria Ludovica von
Bourbon-Spanien

Marie Christine
(1742-1798)
⚭ Albert von
Sachsen-Teschen

Maria Antonia
(1755-1793)
⚭ Ludwig XVI.
von Frankreich

Ferdinand
(1754-1806)
⚭ Maria Beatrix von
Modena-Este

und weitere
sechs Geschwister

Josef II.
(1741-1790)
Kaiser 1765
⚭ 1. Isabella von
Bourbon Parma
⚭ 2. Maria Josefa
von Bayern

Maximilian
(1756-1801)
Kurfürst von
Köln-Münster

Maria Amalia
(1746-1804)
⚭ Ferdinand
von Parma

Maria Anna
(1738-1789)

Maria Elisabeth
(1743-1808)

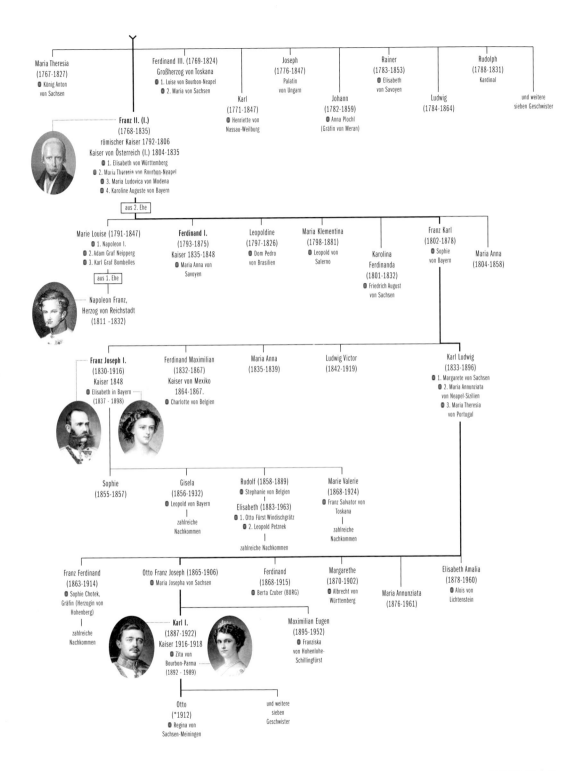

Maria Theresia
(1767-1827)
⚭ König Anton
von Sachsen

Ferdinand III. (1769-1824)
Großherzog von Toskana
⚭ 1. Luise von Bourbon-Neapel
⚭ 2. Maria von Sachsen

Karl
(1771-1847)
⚭ Henriette von
Nassau-Weilburg

Joseph
(1776-1847)
Palatin
von Ungarn

Johann
(1782-1859)
⚭ Anna Plochl
(Gräfin von Meran)

Rainer
(1783-1853)
⚭ Elisabeth
von Savoyen

Ludwig
(1784-1864)

Rudolph
(1788-1831)
Kardinal

und weitere
sieben Geschwister

Franz II. (I.)
(1768-1835)
römischer Kaiser 1792-1806
Kaiser von Österreich (I.) 1804-1835
⚭ 1. Elisabeth von Württemberg
⚭ 2. Maria Theresia von Bourbon-Neapel
⚭ 3. Maria Ludovica von Modena
⚭ 4. Karoline Auguste von Bayern

aus 2. Ehe

Marie Louise (1791-1847)
⚭ 1. Napoleon I.
⚭ 2. Adam Graf Neipperg
⚭ 3. Karl Graf Bombelles

Ferdinand I.
(1793-1875)
Kaiser 1835-1848
⚭ Maria Anna von
Savoyen

Leopoldine
(1797-1826)
⚭ Dom Pedro
von Brasilien

Maria Klementina
(1798-1881)
⚭ Leopold von
Salerno

Karolina
Ferdinanda
(1801-1832)
⚭ Friedrich August
von Sachsen

Franz Karl
(1802-1878)
⚭ Sophie
von Bayern

Maria Anna
(1804-1858)

aus 1. Ehe

Napoleon Franz,
Herzog von Reichstadt
(1811 –1832)

Franz Joseph I.
(1830-1916)
Kaiser 1848
⚭ Elisabeth in Bayern
(1837 - 1898)

Ferdinand Maximilian
(1832-1867)
Kaiser von Mexiko
1864-1867.
⚭ Charlotte von Belgien

Maria Anna
(1835-1839)

Ludwig Victor
(1842-1919)

Karl Ludwig
(1833-1896)
⚭ 1. Margarete von Sachsen
⚭ 2. Maria Annunziata
von Neapel-Sizilien
⚭ 3. Maria Theresia
von Portugal

Sophie
(1855-1857)

Gisela
(1856-1932)
⚭ Leopold von Bayern

zahlreiche
Nachkommen

Rudolf (1858-1889)
⚭ Stephanie von Belgien

Elisabeth (1883-1963)
⚭ 1. Otto Fürst Windischgrätz
⚭ 2. Leopold Petznek

zahlreiche Nachkommen

Marie Valerie
(1868-1924)
⚭ Franz Salvator von
Toskana

zahlreiche
Nachkommen

Franz Ferdinand
(1863-1914)
⚭ Sophie Chotek,
Gräfin (Herzogin von
Hohenberg)

zahlreiche
Nachkommen

Otto Franz Joseph (1865-1906)
⚭ Maria Josepha von Sachsen

Karl I.
(1887-1922)
Kaiser 1916-1918
⚭ Zita von
Bourbon-Parma
(1892 - 1989)

Ferdinand
(1868-1915)
⚭ Berta Czuber (BURG)

Maximilian Eugen
(1895-1952)
⚭ Franziska
von Hohenlohe-
Schillingfürst

Margarethe
(1870-1902)
⚭ Albrecht von
Württemberg

Maria Annunziata
(1876-1961)

Elisabeth Amalia
(1878-1960)
⚭ Alois von
Lichtenstein

Otto
(*1912)
⚭ Regina von
Sachsen-Meiningen

und weitere
sieben
Geschwister

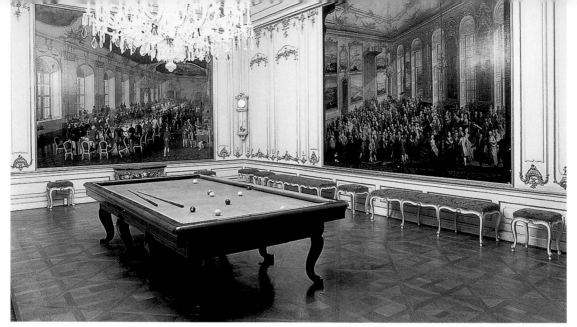

Billiard Room

III. Tour of the palace

From 1779, that is, while Maria Theresa was still alive, both the gardens and the ceremonial rooms of the palace were opened to the public free of charge, provided that "the Court was not in residence and an appointment had been arranged with the palace administration".

Today the ceremonial rooms as well as the private apartments on the *piano nobile* of the palace are open to the public. Visitors enter the lofty columned halls of the vestibule and proceed to the Blue Staircase in the West Wing which leads up to the magnificent state rooms on the first floor.

West Wing

The space now occupied by the **Blue Staircase** was once the dining room of Joseph I's hunting lodge. It was remodelled by Nikolaus Pacassi around 1745 to create a suitably imposing staircase appropriate to the residence and family home of Maria Theresa as Habsburg monarch. The ceiling fresco painted by the Italian artist Sebastiano Ricci in 1701/02 remained untouched by the remodelling. It repre-

sents the glorification of Joseph, the heir to the throne, as warrior and man of virtue. The name of the staircase derives from the delicate blue wash used for the walls which dates from Maria Theresa's time.

The **Billiard Room** is the first room in the suite of audience chambers and private residential quarters of the penultimate Habsburg emperor, Franz Joseph I. The furnishing and decoration of his apartments conveys an impression of this monarch's world, the professional and private aspects of his daily life at the palace. This included billiards, a very popular game at court, first mentioned in connection with this room in 1837.

The paintings in this room represent major historic events in Habsburg history: the middle painting shows the investment ceremony of the Order of Maria Theresa in 1758, on the left is a banquet in the Great Gallery and on the right Franz Joseph at a banquet in the gardens held to mark the centenary of the order's establishment.

Walnut Room; used by Emperor Franz Joseph as an audience chamber

The **Walnut Room** served Franz Joseph as an audience chamber. Its name derives from the precious walnut panelling of its walls dating to around 1765, when the West Wing was refurbished for Joseph II as co-regent of Maria Theresa following the sudden death of Franz I Stephan. The individual panels are framed with gilded moulding and decorated with gilt rocaille. The remarkable Rococo furnishing of the room includes the ornately-carved and gilded Rococo console tables and the carved chandelier with its 48 branches. One hundred years later Franz Joseph commissioned furniture in neo-Rococo style for this audience chamber.

Here Franz Joseph gave countless audiences to his ministers, court officials and government leaders, and on Mondays and Thursdays any subject in his empire could seek an audience with the emperor. As a result of these audiences, Franz Joseph developed an astonishing memory for names and faces, a faculty he retained right into old age.

Franz Joseph's study

Franz Joseph's study presents a complete contrast to the formal magnificence of the Walnut Room. Its plain, historicist furniture displaying the contemporary bourgeois taste of the 1860/70s suited the modest nature of the emperor. Franz Joseph, who described himself as the foremost public servant of his state, worked tirelessly at his desk in the window embrasure, habitually clad in a drab mouse-grey uniform. The emperor's working day began at 5 am, important and unimportant files alike received the same dedicated attention, evidence of his pronounced sense of order which at times verged on pedantry. While he was working the emperor partook of small meals which he had served to him at his desk among the bundles of files and documents. The portraits by the artist Franz Russ dating to 1863 show Franz Joseph and Elisabeth as young monarchs.

Franz Joseph's bedroom was furnished with the same upholstered furniture as his study in 1868 and was to remain virtually unchanged for the next 50 years until the emperor's death. Over the years however numerous photographs, paintings and mementoes of family members, children and grandchildren came to decorate the room. One of these items was the folding screen decorated with devotional pictures from pilgrimages brought as souvenirs by Katharina Schratt, the emperor's intimate friend. It was Empress Elisabeth herself who set up the contact between this popular star of the Viennese stage and her husband, and she deliberately fostered the friendship so that she could be sure the emperor was provided with company during her continual absences from court.

The very un-imperial furnishing of the bedroom with its iron bed, praying stool and marble washstand equipped with toilet articles from that time bear witness to the daily routine of the thrifty and unassuming emperor, who rose at 4 am every day. After performing his morning ablutions in cold water, Franz Joseph, who was a strict Catholic, said his morning prayers. It was in this Spartan iron bed that the 86-year-old emperor died on 21st November 1916, amid the tumult of the First World War. The painting by Franz Matsch shows him 24 hours after his death. On the way out of the room, in the space behind the panelling of the door embrasure, is the lavatory that was installed for the emperor in 1899.

The **Western Terrace Cabinet** leads into the apartments of Empress Elisabeth. This room contains a painting by the French artist Pierre Benevaux showing Maria Theresa's youngest daughters, Marie Antoinette, later Queen of France, and Maria Josepha.

For Sisi, as Elisabeth was affectionately known by her family, her life as Empress of Austria began at Schönbrunn. After arriving in Vienna on 22nd April 1854 she spent the first night at Schönbrunn before her official festive entry into Vienna took place the following day.

Franz Joseph's bedroom, detail showing the screen decorated with votive pictures from pilgrimages

Emperor Franz Joseph in the full-dress uniform of an Austrian field marshal; oil painting by Franz Xaver Winterhalter. 1865

Empress Elisabeth in a ball gown with diamond stars in her hair; oil painting by Franz Xaver Winterhalter, 1865

Empress Elisabeth's study

The **Stairs Cabinet** served the empress as her study and it was here that she wrote numerous letters, diary entries and her poetry. After the first marital crisis in 1859 Elisabeth fled to Madeira, remaining absent from the court at Vienna for a year, and after her return spent frequent periods at Schönbrunn. She had a spiral staircase – no longer extant – built in her study which led down to the private suite of rooms on the ground floor that were refurbished at the same time. From there the freedom-loving empress, who rejected the strict constraints of court life, could leave the palace at any time without being seen by the guards at the door or the palace watch.

Empress Elisabeth's dressing room

Bedroom of the emperor and empress

The **Dressing Room** was a very important feature of any apartments occupied by Elisabeth, as her beauty and exercise regime dominated her daily routine. The Austrian empress was considered to be one of the greatest beauties in the world, a reputation to which the portraits of her by the artist Franz Xaver Winterhalter had contributed in no small measure.

Special beauty preparations, daily gymnastic exercises and dieting were intended to preserve the slender figure which Elisabeth additionally emphasised by wearing tightly laced clothes. Caring for her magnificent almost ankle-length hair, which she usually wore pinned up in a crown of plaits, took up several hours of each day. Her hairdresser, Franziska Feifalik, became one of her closest confidantes and whenever the situation allowed, was pressed into service to stand in for the shy and retiring empress in public.

The myth of her unfading beauty was established by the empress herself. From the age of thirty she refused to be photographed and took to concealing her face behind a fan in public.

The **marital bedroom of Franz Joseph and Elisabeth** was furnished on the occasion of their marriage in 1854 with blue and white upholstery and hangings and heavy palisander wood furniture, which were probably little to the taste of the extravagant young empress. The bedroom was only used by the couple during the early years of their marriage; soon Elisabeth declined to let her husband into the bedroom or withdrew to her private apartments on the ground floor. Despite this rejection and the many rebuffs he was dealt, Franz Joseph fulfilled his beloved Sisi's every wish. His wife learnt early on how to use the power of her beauty. From the 1870s onwards she was able to lead her own life, travelling extensively, while Franz Joseph grew increasingly lonely in her absence. Elisabeth was assassinated by the Italian anarchist Luigi Lucheni in Geneva on 10th September 1898; her husband continued to idolise her beyond her death.

Marie Antoinette Room with table set for a family dinner

In the **Empress's Salon** the atmosphere is determined by the white and gold panelling, the pale silk wall-hangings and the magnificent neo-Rococo furniture. The clock in front of the mirror has an unusual feature: a mirror-image face on the back, so that the time could be seen in the mirror.

The room contains some notable paintings. The portrait of Maria Antoinette in a fashionable hunting costume is by Joseph Kranzinger, while the other pastel portraits are attributed to the Genevan artist Jean-Ètienne Liotard, for whose work Maria Theresa had an especial fondness. They show the heir to the throne, Joseph, as an eleven-year-old boy, as well as a number of his sisters.

The salon was part of the empress's apartments and was accessed via the Blue Staircase and the empress's antechamber. During the 1860s Elisabeth spent most of the time in Vienna and through her continued presence was able to gain increasing influence over the emperor in political affairs. Thus she was instrumental in bringing about the Compromise with Hungary in 1867, the only time that she availed herself of her role as empress.

The room known as the **Marie Antoinette Room** with its white and gold panelling and wall girandoles or candelabra of Bohemian glass served as the family dining room during Elisabeth's time. The table is laid according to an original model and testifies to the imperial dining culture of that epoch. The name of the room derives from a Gobelin tapestry based on the famous painting by Elisabeth Vigée-Le Brun. It showed the French queen with her three children, and came to Schönbrunn as a gift from Napoleon III. After the end of the monarchy the tapestry reverted to private Habsburg ownership.

The **Children's Room** is hung with portraits of some of Maria Theresa's daughters. Painted around 1765, they show Maria Anna, the oldest daughter, who had a deep interest in the natural sciences, in a dress with a blue bodice; the girl in the lace dress with red bows is Marie Christine, Maria Theresa's favourite daughter, who was the only child allowed to marry the husband of her choice, the Duke of Saxony-Teschen; the once so pretty Maria Elisabeth, in a gold coloured dress embellished with colourful cloth roses, was later disfigured by chicken pox and an enlarged goitre, and was unkindly known in the family as "Goitrous Lizzy"; Maria Amalie, in a red velvet dress with white lace sleeves, was married off to the Duke of Bourbon-Parma, who was five years younger than his bride; Maria Karoline, holding a portrait she painted of her father, was married to Ferdinand, King of the Two Sicilies, and later was responsible for a policy of resistance against Napoleon; Marie Antoinette, in a blue dress with white lace and blue bows, left the Viennese court at the age of 15 to be married to the French Dauphin and reside at Versailles as the future Queen of France. On the left may be seen the bathroom that was installed here for Zita, the last Empress of Austria, in 1917.

The **Breakfast Cabinet** is decorated with floral appliqué-work medallions framed in rocaille, executed by Elisabeth Christine, the mother of Maria Theresa. For many generations in the Habsburg family, it was the custom for the children not only to engage in artistic activities but also to learn a manual trade or craft. Maria Theresa and Franz Stephan encouraged the artistic inclinations of their children, who also contributed to the decoration of several of the rooms at Schönbrunn.

Breakfast Cabinet, flower picture with gilt rocaille frame

Breakfast Cabinet, detail with white and gold panelling and framed flower picture

Yellow Salon with portraits of children by Jean Liotard

The **Yellow Salon** on the garden side of the palace contains the original furniture from the time of Maria Theresa. Referred to as the "yellow-moiré room" in the middle of the 18th century, the whole ensemble has recently been restored to its orginal state. The furniture dating to around 1770 was re-upholstered in a stylistically appropriate fabric and regilded. A typical example of a Maria Theresa interior, the ensemble is complemented by the priceless Louis Seize secretaire, made by the renowned cabinet-maker Adam Weisweiler. This lady's writing table is the only memento of Marie Antoinette, executed as queen of France in 1793, that was returned to Vienna after her death. Of note are the numerous pastels of bourgeois children by the Genevan artist Liotard, which Maria Theresa herself purchased. They form a stark contrast to the typically formal court portraits of her own children.

The **Balcony Room** contains portraits of Maria Theresa's children by artists from the school of the court painter Martin van Meytens. Of especial interest is the large-scale painting dated 1751/52 showing the archdukes Joseph, Carl Joseph and Peter Leopold, who had been made regimental commanders-in-chief while still children.

Joseph, aged approximately eleven, is depicted as the commander-in-chief of a dragoons regiment, but his clothing is adapted to official court dress. Carl Joseph (right) is depicted in the uniform of his Hungarian infantry regiment, and Leopold (left) as a miniature cuirassier.

Louis Seize secretaire by Adam Weisweiler, c. 1780

Mirrors Room

The **Mirrors Room** – also called the Hall of Mirrors from 1762 onwards – with its magnifcent white and gold decoration and crystal mirrors is one of the typical state rooms from the epoch of Maria Theresa. Walls and ceiling are decorated with gilt rocaille interspersed with large integral mirrors framed by ormulu girandoles: a Rococo ensemble dating from around 1755 and the setting for audiences and lesser festivities.

It was probably in this room that Leopold Mozart and his children, eleven-year-old Anna and six-year-old Wolfgang, attended a reception in the presence of Empress Maria Theresa on 13th October 1762. The young Wolfgang performed on the "clavecin" or harpsichord for the empress, and afterwards, as his proud father reported, "he sprang up onto her lap, flung his arms round her neck and planted a firm kiss on her cheek."

Large Rosa Room

Central Wing

The three **Rosa Rooms,** a spatial unit consisting of one large and two smaller rooms created in 1763/64, are named after the artist Joseph Rosa, who was commissioned by Maria Theresa to paint the 15 large-scale landscapes set into the walls of this room. The first painting on the right in the Large Rosa Rooom shows the ancestral seat of the dynasty, the Habichtsburg – later corrupted into Habsburg – in the Aargau in Switzerland as an idealised ruin. The painting was no doubt intended to display Maria Theresa's interest in the history of the Habsburg dynasty. The other paintings depict idealised river and mountain landscapes with peasant figures as well as resting flocks of goats and sheep, scenes which contrast with the typical court Rococo decoration in white and gold tones. Interspersed among the gilt stucco decoration of the Large Rosa Room with its playful rocaille work are various musical instruments, probably indicating that this was also used as a music room. The room also contains the portrait of Maria Theresa as Queen of Hungary by Martin van Meytens.

In the second of the smaller Rosa Rooms the visitor can see the so-called Kaunitz Stairs. Count Kaunitz, Maria Theresa's State Chancellor and one of her closest advisors, had an apartment on the floor above, and these stairs allowed him direct access to the *piano nobile*.

The **Lantern Room** with its marble door frames from the time of Joseph I was where the lantern-bearers used to wait in the days before the palace was electrified, in order to light the way for members of the imperial family or the court household after dark.

The **Great Gallery,** with a length of 43 metres and a width of almost ten metres, provided the perfect setting for court festivities. Here balls and grand receptions were held and festive banquets took place. Maria Theresa particularly enjoyed celebrating the name days of family members, on which occasions there was usually a ball as well as theatre and ballet performances given by her own children. In day-to-day court life, this huge room was used as an antechamber where visitors waited before being admitted to audiences with the emperor and empress in the East Wing.

Since the foundation of the Republic in 1918, in keeping with its tradition, the Great Gallery has been used for concerts and receptions. In 1961 the room witnessed the historic encounter between the American president John F. Kennedy and the Soviet premier Nikita Khrushchev.

The white and gold stucco decoration, the tall crystal glass mirrors and the ceiling frescoes of the Great Gallery constitute a total work of art. Created around 1760 by Nikolaus Pacassi in collaboration with the artist Gregorio Guglielmi and the stuccateur Albert Bolla, this festival hall in Rococo style is one of the most magnificent interiors among all European palaces. Between the pilasters the room opens up towards the Parade Court through lofty arches and on the other side through arcades to the Small Gallery, with gold-framed mirrors in between. The magnificent gold stucco decoration seemingly dissolves the boundary between wall and ceiling, gilded floral garlands and weightless consoles leading into the vaults of the frescoed ceiling which are linked to each other with three-dimensional trophies and heraldic motifs.

The ceiling frescoes by the Italian artist Guglielmi are allegories with obvious references to the political, military and economic situation of the times.

Despite the war with Prussia that was being fought at the time, the central fresco dating to 1760 represents the prosperity of the monarchy under the rule of Maria Theresa, who is enthroned at the centre with Franz Stephan and surrounded by the personified virtues of Prudentia (Prudence), Fortitudo (Fortitude) and Justitia (Justice). Around this group range the allegories of the Crown Lands of the Habsburg empire together with their riches, with the hovering figure of Mercury as intermediary between the divine and profane realms.

The fresco at the western end of the room, painted one year later, depicts an allegory of Peace, representing the flourishing of the Crown Lands, promoted by Concordia (Concord) at the zenith of the fresco, surrounded by Abundantia (Abundance) and Pax (Peace).

The fresco depicting a martial allegory at the eastern end of the room fell victim to a direct hit from a bomb in April 1945, during the last days of the Second World War in Europe, and was replaced by a copy in 1947/48. At the centre of the fresco is Mars, the god of war, mounted on a grey horse, and below him Minerva, the goddess of the martial arts. She is also enthroned above an impressively rendered scene depicting a lesson at the Military Academy founded by Maria Theresa. The rest of the fresco represents the three branches of the army – infantry, cavalry and artillery.

The original illumination of the Great Gallery, with countless candles reflected in the former glossy white finish of the walls, was replaced by electricity in 1901, necessitating the installation of 1,104 lightbulbs.

Great Gallery

Small Gallery

The **Small Gallery** was decorated at the same time as the Great Gallery and during Maria Theresa's time served as the setting for small-scale celebrations in the imperial family. During renovation work around 1870 the former white and pink stucco marbling on the walls was removed and replaced by a glossy white finish with elaborate white and gold stucco work in neo-Rococo style. The ceiling fresco, also by Gregorio Guglielmi, was not affected by these alterations. It is again an allegory, this time glorifying the wise and benevolent rule of the House of Habsburg in Austria. At its centre is Aeternitas (immortality) characterised by the hoop of eternity, holding the archducal coronet over a white crane held by Chronos. At her feet Mars, the god of war, forms the central focus. In a protective fold of his cloak lies the she-wolf with the twins Romulus and Remus, together with the S.P.Q.R. standard, a reference to the Roman origins of the empire and thus also an allusion to Franz I Stephan as Roman-German emperor. On the shorter, right-hand side is the figure of an old man wearing a laurel wreath as the personification of the Holy Roman Empire. Around him are the imperial crown, sceptre, orb, banner and Golden Fleece, while a winged genius shows him the philosophers' stone. On the opposite side is a scene alluding to Maria Theresa's virtues of clemency and justice, personified in the figures of Clementia with flames at her brow pointing to a tablet with the inscription *Regnum me comite (eri)t (iust)um (Let my rule be just)*. Facing her is Justitia enthroned, characterised by her attributes of scales and sword.

The Small Gallery opens out through large doors onto the Great Parterre of the gardens, with a view of the Gloriette on the crown of Schönbrunn Hill.

To either side of the Small Gallery are the **Chinese Cabinets** – on the left the Oval Chinese Cabinet and on the right the Round Chinese Cabinet. Both rooms have a distinctly intimate character and were used by Maria Theresa for small social gatherings, for example for playing cards. Before the rooms were decorated and furnished with chinoiseries, the Round Cabinet was used as a small conference room, in which the so-called "Tables de Conspiration" took place. These were secret conferences at which meals were served to the participants by means of a moveable table winched up from the room on the floor below, so that they would not be disturbed or eavesdropped upon by the servants.

The two cabinets were decorated and furnished with precious chinoiseries around 1760, and testify to the predilection and admiration for oriental lacquerwork, silk wall hangings and porcelain that started in the early 18th century and had an increasing influence on styles of interior decoration in the princely palaces of Europe.

Maria Theresa was especially fond of these chinoiseries and they were incorporated into several rooms at Schönbrunn. The Chinese Cabinets have white panelling with elaborately gilded rocaille work. Between the mirrors Chinese lacquer panels of various shapes and sizes are set into the walls and painted with landscapes, flowers and birds. Out of their gilded frames grow small consoles which support figures, vases and other vessels of blue and white porcelain.

Another noteworthy feature in these rooms are the fire-gilt Rococo chandeliers with their enamel candle sockets and holders, as well as the precious intarsia flooring made of various richly-grained exotic and indigenous woods.

Oval Chinese Cabinet

Round Chinese Cabinet, detail with lid handle of a Chinese lidded vase

Ladies' Carousel, oil painting by Martin van Meytens, 1743

The **Carousel Room** served as a waiting room for audiences with Maria Theresa and her husband Franz Stephan of Lorraine. One of the paintings hung here gave the room its name: the Lady's Carriage Parade or Carousel, which took place at the Winter Riding School of the Hofburg in 1743. This event was organised to celebrate the withdrawal from Bohemia of the French and Bavarian forces that had threatened Maria Theresa's position after the death of her father, Charles VI. The young monarch is portrayed riding on a grey horse and leading the riders' quadrille. She is followed by others in small silver-gilt carriages exquisitely carved as shells, of which one example has been preserved in the Wagenburg collection.

The painting depicting the investiture of the Order of St Stephen records another important event in the reign of Maria Theresa. The two portraits, of Charles VI and Joseph II in boyhood, show their subjects in sumptuous Spanish coat-dress.

Hall of Ceremonies

The adjoining **Hall of Ceremonies** was not only used as a second antechamber by Franz Stephan but also as a festival hall for family occasions such as christenings, birthdays and name days, weddings of members of the court household who were of noble birth, as well as for court banquets. The interior decoration of the room, which dates to 1760, includes the magnificent rocaille work, enhanced by three-dimensional ornamentation on the vaulting. The gilt stucco decoration on the white-panelled walls was the work of Albert Bolla, who was also responsible for the decoration of the Great Gallery. The hall was earlier known as the "Battaglia Room", after the decoration on the vaulting in the form of spears, trophies, banners and other appurtenances of war, a symbolic representation of the power of the monarchy.

The Hall of Ceremonies is most remarkable for the monumental paintings commissioned by Maria Theresa. The cycle of paintings represents a socio-political and family event, the marriage of Joseph, the heir to the throne, to Isabella of Parma, who was a member of the royal house of Bourbon, in 1760. Like most of the marriages entered into by Maria Theresa's children, this was a calculated political move on the empress's part, undertaken in order to ensure France's support for Austria. The largest painting shows the entry of the Parma princess on 5th October 1760 against the backdrop of the Vienna Hofburg. The huge, imaginary space in front of the Hofburg provides space for 94 six-horse coaches, and the end of the procession is brought up by the golden coach of the nuptial ambassador, Prince Liechtenstein, together with the blue and silver bridal coach carrying Isabella which is escorted by the imperial Swiss guards in black and yellow uniforms. The other paintings show the marriage ceremony in the Augustinerkirche, the Hofburg parish church, the wedding banquet in the large antechamber of the Hofburg, and finally the Souper and the Serenade in the Redoutensaal ballroom. The luncheon banqueting table in the Hofburg, decked with a new gold service, was set up in a U-shape, and seated at its head were Franz Stephan and Maria Theresa, at their sides the bride and bridegroom followed by the rest of the imperial family. The orchestra in the foreground provided music to accompany the banquet, which was served by members of the high nobility in coat-dress.

Detail from the luncheon banquet held for the wedding of Crown Prince Joseph and Isabella of Parma; in the foreground on the left is a bread roll known as an 'imperial'

Detail from the serenade in the Redoutensaal ballroom; among the onlookers is the young Mozart

For the evening banquet in the Redoutensaal ballroom, the dessert table is laid with a porcelain service. The inside of the U-shaped table is decorated with a long centrepiece made of coloured sugar, representing a garden peopled with numerous figures. A few days later the Serenade took place in the Redouten ballrooms, at which the imperial family sat in the first row.

The most impressive feature of these paintings apart from their scale is the rendering of the details of the buildings, people and their clothing, right down to the tableware. During the years of work that these paintings required in the studio of van Meytens, a tiny portrait of the young Mozart was added to the rows of onlookers in the last painting mentioned above. The child prodigy had been the talk of the town since his legendary performance before the imperial family at Schönbrunn.

This cycle of paintings also includes what is probably the most famous portrait of Maria Theresa, resplendent in a precious gown made of Mechelin lace, as "first lady of Europe".

Rösselzimmer with the Marshals' Table

From the Hall of Ceremonies the visitor can see into the **Rössel** or **Stallions' Room,** with the so-called Marshals' Table. Reconstructed on the basis of a historical model, this festively-decked table was laid for the highest-ranking military officers and holders of court offices, but not dinners which were attended by the emperor. The name of the room derives from the equine portraits dating to the era of the dowager empress Wilhelmine Amalia which were rehung during the refurbishment that took place around 1760. The unique ensemble, comp-

lemented by the large-scale painting of a hunt attended by Joseph I near Marchegg, testifies to the important role played by the horse in court life. Elegant horses, bred from impeccable pedigrees at the imperial studs, were considered the expression of aristocratic lifestyle and courtly splendour.

Blue Chinese Salon

East Wing

The **Blue Chinese Salon** marked the beginning of the private residential apartments of Franz I Stephan. Originally decorated only with walnut panelling, the room was hung with precious Chinese rice-paper wall-hangings in 1806. Made in the middle of the 18th century, these wall-hangings were probably acquired by Maria Theresa in her enthusiasm for chinoiseries and then put into storage and not used until the reign of Emperor Franz II/I, when they were hung in five separate rooms at Schönbrunn. However, only those used to decorate the Blue Chinese Salon have survived. The rice-paper hangings display floral motifs on a pale background. Vertically arranged panels contain

alternating oval and rectangular fields with scenic representations on a blue ground painted with precious azurite. The scenes, executed in black China ink and bronze paint, are intended to illustrate for the European onlooker four activities that were important in the Chinese world: silkworm breeding and silk production, rice growing, the manufacturing of porcelain and the cultivation of tea. These pictures are contained within framing motifs of flowers or bamboo, while above them are baskets filled with flowers, surrounded by birds, butterflies and insects.

Blue Chinese Salon, detail of the wallpaper: a customer inspects a tea-leaf in the presence of the vendor

The tables with their valuable inlays of semi-precious stones in black marble are also worthy of note.

It was here in this room that the negotiations with the last Austrian emperor, Karl I, took place which ultimately led to his renouncing the affairs of government on 11th November 1918. The next day the Republic was proclaimed, thus ending Schönbrunn's history as an imperial residence.

The **Vieux-Laque Room** was remodelled by Maria Theresa as a memorial room to her much-loved husband, Franz Stephan, followng his sudden death. The precious and extravagantly expensive decoration with black lacquer panels from the imperial manufactory in Peking was probably carried out to designs by the architect Isidor Canevale. Originally produced as folding screens for the European market, these lacquer panels were cut down and incorporated into the walnut panelling. The walls and doors, the latter crowned by supraportas, are articulated by vertical sections with elaborately carved and gilded framing, while the lacquer panels set into them are painted with genre scenes, landscapes and representations of flowers and birds. The framing decoration already heralds the transition from Rococo to early Classicism.

Of particular interest are the portraits that Maria Theresa commissioned especially for the memorial room. The posthumous portrait of Franz Stephan was painted by Pompeo Batoni, who also executed the dual portrait of Joseph II and his brother Leopold. This painting was done in Rome in 1769, when the two brothers were staying there on the occasion of the papal election. On the table in front of Joseph lies the *Esprit des lois* by Montesquieu, one of the major works of the Enlightenment, whose ideas permeated the young emperor's thinking and all his political endeavours. The third painting by Anton von Maron shows Leopold's wife, Maria Ludovica of Spain, together with three of their numerous children. The small portrait shows Maria Theresa in mourning; after her husband's death she wore mourning for the rest of her life.

The floor in this room is also of the very finest quality, remarkable not only for the choice woods and design, but also on account of the various hues and shading together with the resulting optical effects.

Vieux-Laque Room

The Duke of Reichstadt as gardener; oil painting by Carl von Sales, c. 1815

The **Napoleon Room** was used by Napoleon Bonaparte as his bedroom in 1805 and again in 1809. He occupied Vienna twice, making his head-quarters at Schönbrunn on each occasion. His marriage to Marie Louise, daughter of the reigning emperor Franz II/I, in 1810 was intended to seal the peace between the two rulers. Later on this room was occupied by Napoleon's son, the Duke of Reichstadt. Baptised Napoleon Franz and given the title King of Rome, he came to Vienna at the age of two, following the defeat and abdication of his father, and grew up at his maternal grandfather's court, enjoying a sheltered upbringing with little contact with the outside world. He had botany lessons and was instructed in the arts of gardening. The painting shows him as a boy in the park at Laxenburg working in the garden. He died of consumption in 1832 at the age of 21; the bust shows him on his death bed. Mementoes of him include his beloved pet, a crested lark.

Porcelain Room

The **Porcelain Room,** refurbished in 1763/64 to designs by Jean Pillement, a French artist active at the Viennese court, served Maria Theresa as a games room and study. Blue and white wooden framework, carved and painted in imitation of porcelain, covers the small room right up to the ceiling. The wall panelling is articulated by garlands of flowers and fruit that rise from a balustrade and are held together by Chinese parasols. In between are 213 blue Chinese ink drawings with Chinese genre scenes, which were executed by Franz Stephan and his children. The decoration also includes four framed portrait medallions of Marie Christine and her husband Albert of Saxony-Teschen, Isabella of Parma, the first wife of Crown Prince Joseph, and of the emperor himself.

Porcelain Room, portrait medallion of Marie Christine

Millions Room

The so-called **Millions Room** received its name from the wall panelling of a precious exotic type of rosewood, which has an exceptionally fine figured surface resulting in beautiful aesthetic effects. The whole interior was originally made for the Belvedere Palace and was transferred to Schönbrunn in 1766 on the orders of Maria Theresa. Set into the wooden panelling are Indo-Persian miniatures from the 17th century, framed in delicate gilt rocaille work. In order to fit the miniatures into the frames, the miniatures were partly cut down to size and reassembled into new compositions by members of the imperial family in a sort of collage technique. The inevitable intervening spaces were concealed with additional painting of land- or skyscapes. The collage of any one individual cartouche can consist of anything up to 27 different individual pieces.

Miniatures Cabinet with table set for breakfast

The miniatures show scenes from the life of Mogul rulers in India in the 16th and 17th centuries. They were taken from a sequence of 61 manuscript leaves originally written for the Mogul court and decorated with illustrations, and they give a uniquely consistent picture of the private and court life of these Indian rulers of Persian extraction.

During the Second World War the panelling of the Millions' Room was dismantled and taken to be stored in the saltmines at Altaussee in order to preserve it from the threat of imminent destruction. In 1980, as the miniatures are extremely sensitive to light, it was decided on grounds of conservation to remove them from the panelling and replace them with high-quality facsimiles. The originals are now stored in the Collection of Manuscripts at the Austrian National Library.

From the Millions' Room the visitor may view the **Miniatures Cabinet,** hung with numerous small pictures, some of them signed, executed by the children and husband of Maria Theresa. The breakfast table is set with 19th-century porcelain from the Thun-Klösterle manufactory, a service that was made for the Prague court of Emperor Ferdinand I, who had abdicated in favour of his nephew Franz Joseph in 1848.

Gobelin Salon, detail showing chair with representations of the months of July and August

Gobelin Salon, detail showing chair with representations of the months of May and June

The room known as the **Gobelin Salon** belonged to the apartments of Franz Joseph's parents from 1837 to 1873. It served Franz Karl, Emperor Ferdinand's brother, and his wife, Sophie, as a drawing-room and was furnished in the typically plain and homely style of the Biedermeier era.

In 1873 the room was completely refurbished and hung with Brussels tapestries from the 18th century showing market and harbour scenes. These were made to designs by David Teniers the Younger, and had been brought to Vienna from the royal palace at Ofen (Budapest).

These tapestries are complemented by the remarkable tapestry-upholstered armchairs displaying representations of the twelve months of the year and the signs of the zodiac, which were added to the room's furnishings at the same time.

Archduchess Sophie's study; water colour by Rudolf von Alt, 1855

The room known as the **Study of Archduchess Sophie** was furnished for Franz Joseph's mother. Driven by ambition, Sophie pursued an energetic and ultimately successful plan to secure the Habsburg throne for her son. She was not only the mother-in-law but also the aunt of Empress Elisabeth; however, the relationship between the two women was always difficult and fraught with conflict. Typical of the era of Franz Joseph, the neo-Rococo interior contains numerous family portraits and mementoes. The only piece of the original furniture to have been preserved is a lady's secretaire with elaborate mother-of-pearl inlay on the lid, which demonstrates the superb quality of Viennese craftsmanship in the 19th century.

In the **Red Salon,** formerly Maria Theresa's library, hang portraits of several Habsburg emperors, starting with Leopold II, who followed his brother Joseph II (1765-1790) on the throne but reigned only briefly (1790-1792). Beside him is his son Franz, who as Franz II was Holy Roman Emperor from 1792. In 1806 he was compelled by the Napoleonic Wars to dissolve the Holy Roman Empire, having erected the Austrian Crown Lands into the Austrian Empire two years previously. Thus the last Holy Roman Emperor Franz II became the first Austrian Emperor Franz I.

Franz II/I (1792-1835) married his eldest daughter Marie Louise to Napoleon, and his second daughter Leopoldine, whose portrait is displayed on the easel, to the Emperor of Brazil. Leopoldine played a major role in the independence movement in Brazil, where she is today still celebrated as a national heroine.

Emperor Franz II/I; oil painting by Friedrich Amerling, 1832

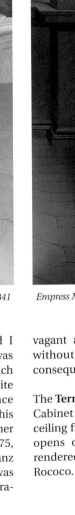

Emperor Ferdinand I.; oil painting by Leopold Kupelwieser, 1841

Empress Maria Anna; oil painting by Leopold Kupelwieser, c. 1841

The other portraits show Emperor Ferdinand I (1835-1848) and his wife Maria Anna. Ferdinand was the eldest son of Emperor Franz II/I, and as such had to follow his father on the throne, despite having suffered from serious ill-health since childhood. In 1848 he abdicated in favour of his nephew Franz Joseph and retired to Prague together with his wife. He died there without issue in 1875, bequeathing his enormous private fortune to Franz Joseph as sole heir. From then on, Franz Joseph was possessed of sufficient means to fund the extra-vagant and costly lifestyle of his wife, Elisabeth, without having to worry about the financial consequences.

The **Terrace Cabinet,** known from 1775 as the Flower Cabinet after its painted panelling, has a remarkable ceiling fresco. The painted *trompe l'oeil* architecture opens out into a sky populated with putti and rendered in the typically delicate colours of the Rococo.

The so-called **Reiches Zimmer** (lit.: "rich room") was once the bedroom of Franz Joseph's parents, Franz Karl and Sophie, and where he himself was born in 1830. The wallpaper with a printed pattern of foliage, parts of which are still visible, dates from this time.

Exhibited in this room today is the only surviving bed of state from the Viennese court. This magnificent and sumptuously appointed state bed was commissioned for the imperial bedchamber of Maria Theresa's parents, Emperor Charles VI and Elisabeth Christine, in the Favorita, another Habsburg palace in Vienna, but not completed until 1737. Later it passed to the ownership of Maria Theresa and was set up in the so-called "Rich Bedroom" on the *piano nobile* of the Leopoldine Wing of the Vienna Hofburg, which Maria Theresa and her husband Franz Stephan moved into in 1740. As the term "bed of state" indicates, it was a ceremonial attribute rather than an item of furniture in daily use, serving for example as the setting for the baptism of Crown Prince Joseph in 1741. The ornate interior of this bedroom consists of the bed of state with its canopy, counterpane, textile wall panels and curtains, all made of red velvet with precious gold and silver embroidery.

In order to afford this important textile ensemble the greatest possible protection, it is exhibited in a glass showcase, as are also the pastel portraits of Maria Theresa and Franz Stephan.

Reiches Zimmer, detail with Bed of State

Franz Karl's study, detail with pictures by Archduchess Marie Christine

In the **Study of Franz Karl,** once part of the suite of rooms occupied by Franz Joseph's father, the paintings hung here take us back one last time to the era of Maria Theresa. The famous family portrait from the studio of van Meyten dated 1754 shows Emperor Franz Stephan and Maria Theresa with eleven of their sixteen children: Ferdinand Karl, born in June 1754, the 13-year-old Joseph in a red gold coat-dress, turning towards his mother who is wearing a blue satin dress, and Franz Stephan in Spanish coat-dress surrounded by his oldest daughters. Also in this room are likenesses of three women who played an important role in Maria Theresa's life: to the left of the door is her sister, Maria Anna, who died in youth, next to her is their mother, Marie Christine, once famed for her beauty, and Countess Fuchs, Maria Theresa's erstwhile governess and later confidante, the only non-Habsburg to be buried in the imperial crypt. On the opposite wall are small paintings that give an impression of the artistic accomplishments of Maria Theresa's children. These include the family circle celebrating the Feast of St Nicholas and Joseph visiting his beloved spouse Isabella at her lying-in.

The **Hunting Room** is the last room in the tour, providing a reminder of the erstwhile function of Schönbrunn as a hunting lodge. The painting entitled *Partridges at Schönbrunn* by Johann Georg Hamilton shows the palatial hunting lodge built by Fischer von Erlach.

Franz I Stephan and Maria Theresa with their family; oil painting by Martin van Meytens, 1754/55

Suite of rooms in the Goess Apartments

Ground Floor

Between 1769 and 1777, Maria Theresa had a suite of rooms on the ground floor of the palace in the section facing the garden painted with exotic landscape murals. She herself occupied the Goess Apartments to the left of the vestibule, while the other rooms were placed at the disposal of those of her children who were still living at court. Maria Theresa commissioned the paintings from the

Bohemian artist Johann Wenzel for her own apartments, engaging the painter Martin Steinrucker for the rooms intended for her children. The rooms are remarkable for their illusionistic landscape murals which aimed at merging the painted representation of Nature on the walls with the real landscape beyond the windows.

Goess Apartments with exotic murals by Johann Wenzel Bergl

Goess Apartments and Crown Prince Apartments

The Goess Apartments occupied by Maria Theresa constitute a functional and artistically conceived unit of four rooms, whose mural paintings range from untouched exotic landscapes to the formal exactitude of the Baroque garden. In the first two rooms the tropical vegetation teems with exotic waterbirds, peaceful Nature paired with luxuriance and richness, albeit with hints of transiency in the artfully arranged fruits. Spatial emphasis is provided merely by painted portals at the doors, while walls and ceilings merge in the tendrils of the rampant vegetation. The second room is in the style of a formal Baroque garden, the expression of man's mastery of nature, as indicated by silken draperies, a peacock and baskets of fruit. Echoing the real garden outside with its filigree wooden pavilions, the last room is itself a painted pavilion.

The landscapes in the Crown Prince Apartments that extend along the side of the building facing the Meidlinger Kammergarten or Crown Prince Garden are intended to represent indigenous scenes, albeit enhanced with exotic and antique elements.

The 'hands-on' zone on the ground floor of Schönbrunn Palace

Gisela Apartments and "The Schönbrunn Experience"

The Gisela Apartments located on the south-western side of the palace facing the garden consist of two rooms with exotic landscape murals executed by the artists Bergl and Steinrucker, the "Rococo Room" with its weightless *trompe l'oeil* architectural paintings, and two further white and gold rooms in Rococo style. The entire suite of rooms on the western garden side of the palace is today open to the public as a children's museum under the motto of the "Schönbrunn Experience".

The illusionistic landscapes of the Bergl rooms again display exotic motifs combined with naturalistic sections. The landscapes in both rooms are characterised by clear, bright colours. While the landscapes in one room are dominated by exotic flora and fauna, in the other they contain oriental towns with mosques and palaces represented in

stark perspective and are embellished with fragments of antique statues or monuments at the nearer edge of the picture.

Before the landscape rooms is a small oval room which in the time before 1760, during Maria Theresa's reign, was used for laying the so-called "conspiracy table" and from where it was winched up to the room today known as the Chinese Cabinet on the *piano nobile*.

The rooms adjoining the Bergl rooms today provide the setting for a "hands-on" zone for children and adults designed to make everyday imperial life and the history of the palace and its occupants more immediate to the visitor.

The so-called "Rococo Room" provides a special setting with its illusionistic spatial articulation: painted doorways, alcoves with flower vases, a room characterised particularly by its pastel Rococo tones.

The maze; detail with dead end

The garden with the Great Parterre and Maze

According to the Baroque conception of princely palaces, according to which architecture and Nature must interpenetrate, Schönbrunn Palace and its gardens form a unified whole, each element relating to the other in a variety of different ways. The Baroque layout together with the extensions from the last decade of Maria Theresa's life, have been preserved largely unchanged and still dominate the appearance of the gardens and park at Schönbrunn. The Grand Parterre that extends along the median axis of the palace complex to the foot of Schönbrunn Hill, was laid out during the 1770s. Divided into eight sections of different sizes, it is separated from the lateral boskets by clipped formal hedges. These hedges originally boasted shallow alcoves in which numerous mythological statues were placed. Since the early years of the last century they have become increasingly overgrown and the figures are today hardly visible in the round. However, they will in future be returned to their original state.

The maze, adjoining the Great Parterre to the south-west, was laid out before 1720. It was less a maze as such than a meandering path that led to the centre without the customary dead-ends and false turns. Tall and narrow hedges, which were partly covered over, provided a pleasant setting for a gentle stroll. During the 19th century the maze gradually fell into disuse and was ultimately cleared in 1892, as "owing to its density it serves purposes that are prohibited in public parks".

Work was started on the reconstruction of the maze to a design based as far as possible on historical models, and a major part of it is now open to visitors to Schönbrunn.

The maze

The Great Parterre looking towards the Neptune Fountain and Gloriette

The Neptune Fountain; detail with Neptune at the centre of the figural group

The monuments in the park and gardens

While palace and gardens were largely completed by 1770, Schönbrunn Hill as the extension of the Grand Parterre was still little more than a clearing in the trees. It was finally laid out during the last ten years of Maria Theresa's life.

The Neptune Fountain was constructed at the foot of the hill and on its crest the Gloriette was built.

The Neptune Fountain was erected as the crowing element of the Great Parterre in 1776. At the centre of the huge pool rises a rocky landscape populated by the sea-god Neptune and his entourage. At the centre stands Neptune with Thetis kneeling at his feet surrounded by Tritons, creatures that are half man and half fish, with their conch-shell trumpets.

Gloriette; detail with groups of trophies along the lateral flights of stairs

The hieroglyph decoration on the obelisk at the centre of the fountain

The Gloriette, an early Classicistic colonnaded structure, had been built one year previously. The triumphal arch-like central section, which was glazed before Maria Theresa's death, is crowned by a massive imperial eagle perching atop a globe, while the external flights of stairs leading up to the lateral arcades are lined with trophies. The flat roof contained by a balustrade was already being used as a viewing platform by the 19th century.

The terminus of the individual axial paths were each given a *point de vue*. Thus the Obelisk Fountain was constructed to the east as a counterpart ot the menagery pavilion in the west, which had been built in 1759. Rising from the pool is a grotto mount peopled with river gods, enlivened with elaborate water cascades and crowned by a lofty obelisk inscribed with (spurious) hieroglyphs.

Not far from the Obelisk Fountain the Roman Ruins were constructed as a romantic garden setting. The ensemble consists of a pool enclosed by a massive round arch with lateral walls, and creates the impression of an antique building slowly crumbling away into the ground.

The Palm House

The Palm House, Zoo and Wagenburg

The Schönbrunn Palm House, erected on the site of the Botanical Gardens laid out around 1750 by Franz Stephan, houses what was once the imperial botanical collection. In the tripartite glass structure, built in 1881/82 and measuring 113 metres in length, tunnel-like passages create varied climatic zones, fostering the growth of this wealth of exotic plant species.

The Zoo at Schönbrunn, the oldest Baroque zoo still in existence in its original function, was founded like the Botanical Garden by Franz I Stephan in 1752. The keeping of rare and exotic foreign animals had been a luxury indulged in at princely courts as an expression of their rank since the 16th century. The zoo complex at Schönbrunn was laid out in the form of thirteen pens projecting radially from a central pavilion, from where the imperial family and selected guests could observe the rare animals.

This central pavilion, sited at the end of the great western avenue, was remodelled as a memorial room by Maria Theresa following the death of her husband. She had the interior fitted out with walnut panelling embellished with gilt rocaille into which are set large mirrors alternating with portraits of rare animals.

Menagerie pavilion; built in 1759 to designs by Nikolaus Jadot

Wagenburg, imperial carriage

The Wagenburg is a collection of carriages and sleighs, sedan chairs, litters, harnesses and shabraques from the former imperial and royal court carriage fleet, moved here from the Winter Riding School in 1922. This collection features the official state carriages of the Viennese court from many centuries, including the Baroque imperial coach and carriages from the Biedermeier and Classicist eras together with a number from the epoch of Franz Joseph I. Besides masterpieces of Viennese carriage-making the collection also contains three Parisian vehicles, including the famous perambulator built for the Duke of Reichstadt, Napoleon's only son.

Chronology

1311 First documented evidence of a watermill on the site now occupied by Schönbrunn Palace

1569 Emperor Maximilian II purchases the estate, which from then on remains in the possession of the Habsburg dynasty as an institution

1605 Destroyed by Hungarian forces

1612 Discovery of the 'Schöner Brunnen' by Emperor Matthias

From 1637 dowager residence of Eleonore of Gonzaga, wife of Ferdinand II

1642 *Château de plaisance* built for the emperor's widow; first documented mention of Schönbrunn as the name of the estate

From 1657 dowager residence of Eleonore of Mantua of the House of Gonzaga, wife of Ferdinand III

1683 Turkish siege of Vienna and devastation of the deer park and gardens at Schönbrunn

From 1688: preliminary designs by Johann Berhard Fischer von Erlach for a palatial hunting lodge

1696 to 1700 Construction of a hunting lodge for the heir-apparent, Joseph

1711 Death of Joseph I. Until 1728 dowager residence of his wife, Wilhelmine Amalie

1740 Accession to the throne of Maria Theresa following the sudden death of her father, Charles VI

1743 to 1763 Rebuilding and refurbishment of the hunting lodge to create a palatial residence under the supervision of architect Nikolaus Pacassi

1765 Death of Emperor Franz Stephan. Refurbishment of his apartments as memorial rooms

1780 Death of Maria Theresa

1805 and 1809 Schönbrunn occupied by Napoleon

1817 to 1819 Renovation of the palace by Emperor Franz II/I and remodelling of the façade into its present form; façade painted in "Schönbrunn yellow" for the first time

1830 Birth of Franz Joseph at Schönbrunn

1848 Franz Joseph becomes Emperor of Austria

1853/54 Refurbishment of the west wing in preparation for Franz Joseph's impending marriage

1854 Marriage of Franz Joseph to the Wittelsbach princess Elisabeth in Bavaria, known as Sisi

1860s Elisabeth frequently spends extended periods at Schönbrunn

1867 Hungarian Compromise

1889 Suicide of Crown Prince Rudolf at Mayerling

1898 Assassination of Empress Elisabeth in Geneva

1914-1918 First World War

November 1916 Death of Franz Joseph at Schönbrunn after a reign of 68 years

November 1918 Emperor Karl renounces all share in the affairs of state; foundation of the Republic of Austria

Plan of the *piano nobile*

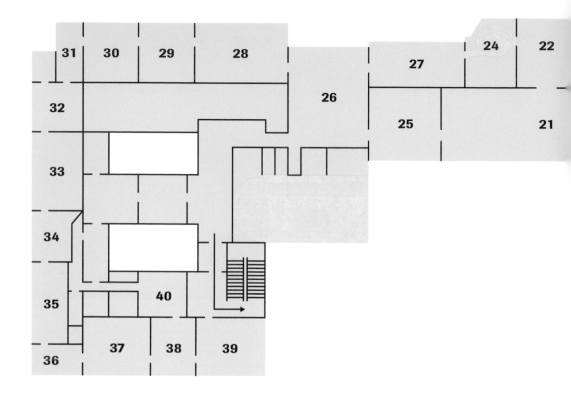

1 Guards Room	11 Marie Antoinette Room
2 Billiard Room	12 Children's Room
3 Walnut Room	13 Breakfast Cabinet
4 Franz Joseph's study	14 Yellow Salon
5 Franz Joseph's bedroom	15 Balcony Room
6 Western Terrace Cabinet	16 Mirrors Room
7 Stairs Cabinet	17 Great Rosa Room
8 Dressing Room	18 First Small Rosa Room
9 Bedroom of Franz Joseph and Elisabeth	19 Second Small Rosa Room
10 Empress's Salon	20 Lantern Room

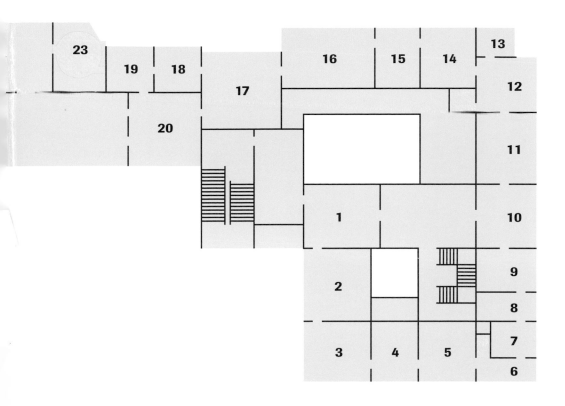

21 Great Gallery
22 Small Gallery
23 Round Chinese Cabinet
24 Oval Chinese Cabinet
25 Carousel Room
26 Hall of Ceremonies
27 Stallions' Room
28 Blue Chinese Salon
29 Vieux-Laque Room
30 Napoleon Room

31 Porcelain Room
32 Millions Room
33 Gobelin Salon
34 Study of Archduchess Sophie
35 Red Salon
36 Terrace Cabinet
37 Reiches Zimmer
38 Study of Franz Karl
39 Salon of Franz Karl
40 Hunting Room

Illustrations

Photographers
A.K.: Alexander Koller
E.K.: Edgar Knaack
F.S.: Fritz Simak
G.F.: Gerhard Fally
G.T.: Gerhard Trumler
J.W.: Johannes Wagner
M.S.: Margherita Spiluttini
P.A.: Photobusiness/Artothek
T.A.: Agentur Anzenberger/Toni Anzenberger

Schloß Schönbrunn Kultur- und Betriebsges.m.b.H.
2/3 A.K., 4 A.K., 5 J.W., 6 J.W., 7 F.S., 10 A.K., 11 A.K.,
12 G.T., 13 A.K., 14 P.A., 15 P.A., 16 J.W., 17li. A.K.,
17re. A.K., 18 A.K., 19o. A.K., 19u. A.K., 20o. A.K.,
20u. A.K., 21 A.K., 22 G.T., 24/25 A.K., 26 M.S.,
27o. A.K.,27u. A.K., 28, 29 A.K., 30o. A.K., 30u. E.K.,
31 A.K., 32 A.K., 33 A.K., 34/35 A.K., 36 E.K., 37o. A.K.,
37u. A.K.,38 A.K., 39 A.K., 40li. A.K., 40re. A.K.,
41, 42 E.K., 45 M.S., 46 A.K., 47 F.S., 48 A.K., 49 A.K.,
50o. G.F., 50u. G.F., 51o. G.F., 51li.u. G.F., 51re.u. G.F.,
52o. G.F., 52u. G.F., 53o. G.F., 53u. G.F., 54 T.A., 55 T.A.,
56o. A.K., 56u. G.T., 57li. A.K., 57re. A.K., 58 A.K.,
59o. A.K., 59u. A.K.

Kunsthistorisches Museum, Wien
43li., 43re.

Schönbrunn Palace
Guide to the Palace

ISBN 3-905168-30-1
NE: Elfriede Iby

First published March 2003

Designed and typeset by Atelier Olschinsky
Printed by Alpina Druck GmbH/Innsbruck, Austria
Translated by Sophie Kidd

Copyright © 2003 Schloss Schönbrunn
Kultur- und Betriebsges.m.b.H., Wien

Bibliography

Corti, Egon Caesar Conte/Sokol Hans.
Kaiser Franz Joseph. Im Abendglanz einer Epoche.
Graz-Vienna-Cologne 1990

Dernjač, Josef. Zur Geschichte von Schönbrunn.
Vienna 1885

Eigl, Kurt/Hubmann Franz. Schönbrunn. Ein Schloß
und seine Welt. Vienna-Munich-Zurich-Innsbruck 1980

Freudenreich, Ernst. Das k.k. Lustschloß Schönbrunn,
dessen Geschichte, sowie Erläuterungen über die im
Bereich des Parkes errichteten Bau- und Bildhauer-
werke. Vienna 1873

Glaser, Josef. Schönbrunner Chronik. 5th ed., revised,
Vienna 1990

Hajós, Géza. Schönbrunn. Wiener Geschichtsbücher.
Vol. 18. Vienna-Hamburg 1976

Iby, Elfriede/Koller, Alexander. Schönbrunn. Vienna 2000

Kugler, Georg. Schloß Schönbrunn. Die Prunkräume.
Vienna 1995

Leitner, Quirin. Monographie des kaiserlichen Lust-
schlosses Schönbrunn. Vienna 1875

Maria Theresia und ihre Zeit. Zur 200. Wiederkehr des
Todestages. Exhibition catalogue. Vienna 1980

Ottillinger, Eva B./Hanzl, Lieselotte. Kaiserliche Inte-
rieurs. Die Wohnkultur des Wiener Hofes im 19. Jahr-
hundert. Vienna-Cologne-Weimar 1997

Raschauer, Oskar. Schönbrunn. Der Schlossbau Kaiser
Josefs I. Vienna 1960

Vocelka, Karl/Heller Lynne. Die Lebenswelt der Habs-
burger. Kultur- und Mentalitätsgeschichte einer Familie.
Graz-Vienna-Cologne 1997

Weissenbacher, Gerhard. Hietzing. Architektur
und Geschichte eines Wiener Gemeindebezirkes.
Vol. 1. Vienna 1996